D1105499

8/11

PLAY BALL
BASEBALL

PITCHER

By Jason Glaser

Gareth Stevens
Publishing

Please visit our Web site, www.garethstevens.com. For a free color catalog of all our high-quality books, call toll free 1-800-542-2595 or fax 1-877-542-2596.

Library of Congress Cataloging-in-Publication Data

Glaser, Jason.
Pitcher / Jason Glaser.
    p. cm. — (Play ball. Baseball)
Includes index.
ISBN 978-1-4339-4496-3 (pbk.)
ISBN 978-1-4339-4497-0 (6-pack)
ISBN 978-1-4339-4495-6 (library binding)
1. Pitching (Baseball)—Juvenile literature. 2. Pitchers (Baseball)—Juvenile literature. I. Title.
GV871.G63 2011
796.357'22—dc22

                                2010039136

First Edition

Published in 2011 by
Gareth Stevens Publishing
111 East 14th Street, Suite 349
New York, NY 10003

Copyright © 2011 Gareth Stevens Publishing

Designer: Michael J. Flynn
Editor: Greg Roza

Photo credits: Cover, pp. 1, 22, 24 Jim McIsaac/Getty Images; (cover, back cover, pp. 2–3, 5, 7, 11, 17, 35, 44–48 stadium background), pp. 40 (all), 41, 42 Shutterstock.com; p. 4 John G. Zimmerman/ Sports Illustrated/Getty Images; p. 5 Patrick A. Burns/Archive Photos/Getty Images; p. 7 Transcendental Graphics/Getty Images; p. 8 Chicago History Museum/Archive Photos/Getty Images; p. 9 Stan Wayman/ Time & Life Pictures/Getty Images; p. 10 Photo File/Archive Photos/Getty Images; p. 11 FPG/ Archive Photos/Getty Images; p. 12 New York Times Co./Archive Photos/Getty Images; pp. 13, 16 Al Messerschmidt/Getty Images; p. 14 Bernstein Associates/Getty Images; p. 15 Otto Greule Jr./ Getty Images; p. 17 Fort Worth Star-Telegram/McClatchy-Tribune/Getty Images; pp. 18, 21 Jonathan Daniel/Getty Images; pp. 19, 38 Kevin C. Cox/Getty Images; p. 20 Mike Zarrilli/ Getty Images; p. 23 J. Meric/Getty Images; pp. 24, 37 Ezra Shaw/Getty Images; p. 25 John W. McDonough/Sports Illustrated/Getty Images; p. 26 Garrett Ellwood/Getty Images; p. 27 G. Newman Lowrance/Getty Images; p. 28 Ron Vesely/Getty Images; p. 29 Jeff Gross/Getty Images; p. 30 Chris McGrath/Getty Images; p. 31 Christian Petersen/Getty Images; p. 32 Nick Laham/ Getty Images; p. 33 Michael Ivins/Boston Red Sox/Getty Images; p. 34 Al Bello/Getty Images; p. 35 Mike Stobe/Getty Images; p. 36 Mitchell Layton/Getty Images; p. 39 Damian Strohmeyer/ Sports Illustrated/Getty Images; p. 43 iStockphoto.com; p. 45 Jed Jacobsohn/Getty Images.

Printed in the United States of America

CPSIA compliance information: Batch #CW11GS: For further information contact Gareth Stevens, New York, New York at 1-800-542-2595.

CONTENTS

Boldface words appear in the glossary.

Today's Hero

Every day is a new day for a pitcher. A great game one day is quickly forgotten with a bad outing the next. Likewise, yesterday's battered pitcher often becomes today's hero.

Bitter Rivalry

In the 1950s, the Brooklyn Dodgers and New York Yankees shared a city but little else. They were powerful rivals who had met in several World Series. The Dodgers were reigning champs when they met the Yankees in the 1956 World Series. After four games the series was tied 2–2.

Game 2 of the 1956 World Series, shown here, was played at Ebbets Field in Brooklyn. The Dodgers won 13-8.

Perfection

The Yankee pitcher who had lost Game 2 badly, Don Larsen, was back to pitch in Game 5. This time, batter by batter, inning by inning, Larsen threw the Dodgers out. Their few hit balls were thrown out by Larsen's teammates. In the end, 27 batters stepped up, and 27 sat down. Larsen had redeemed himself by pitching a **perfect game**—the only one in World Series history—and helping the Yankees toward another championship.

Even though Larsen didn't get everyone out by himself, he put nearly every play in motion. Let's look at how pitchers arm themselves for games.

Larsen throws a
pitch during Game 5
of the World Series.

5

01 Pitching's Past

In the beginning, pitchers were supposed to help the batter hit. As teams looked for new ways to win games, the pitcher became a weapon rather than just a ball server.

No Nonsense

In the 1850s, a pitcher's job was to put a ball over home plate where the batter could hit it. Curveballs and hard-thrown fastballs were considered unsportsmanlike. Still, pitchers who could throw special pitches won more ball games, so teams wanted such pitchers on their side. In time, pitchers began trying to get every batter out.

Changing Rules

Rules change whenever the advantage between pitchers and batters gets out of balance. A pitcher's mound was added and changed, and the **strike zone** has grown both larger and smaller over the years.

6

Fastballs were so hard to hit that the rules changed in 1893 to move the pitcher's mound from 50 feet (15.2 m) away from home plate to 60 feet 6 inches (18.4 m) away. The extra distance gave batters more time to react, and they started hitting the ball more often. In response, pitchers began scuffing the ball, spitting on it, and doing anything they could to change the ball's surface. A messy ball didn't fly straight and was harder to hit.

Burleigh Grimes demonstrates how to prepare a spitball. Grimes was the last professional pitcher allowed to throw the spitball.

Scuffed balls were so wild that not even the pitchers knew where they would go. When one hit and killed a batter in 1920, all altered balls became illegal. Pitchers had to learn some new tricks to fool batters. By holding, gripping, or spinning the ball differently, pitchers invented pitches—like the knuckleball and slider—that are still used today.

Although some say it was invented a few years earlier, most people credit Eddie Cicotte with inventing the knuckleball in 1908.

Two pitchers for the
Cleveland Indians warm up in
the "bull pen" in 1955.

Pitching Rotation

Originally, pitchers threw for the entire game and often came back to pitch in the next game. Their pitches got easier to hit as the games and seasons got longer. Teams began using relief pitchers to finish off a game when the starting pitchers got tired. They also kept more pitchers on a team so players could rest more days between starts. Using fresh arms kept batters from getting more hits.

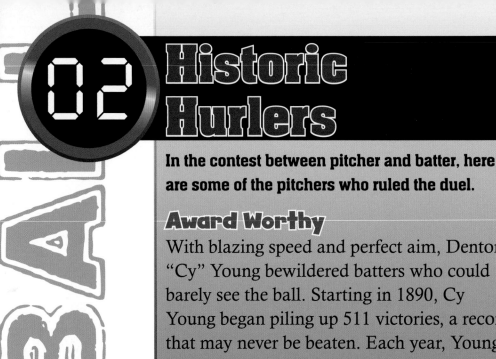

02 Historic Hurlers

In the contest between pitcher and batter, here are some of the pitchers who ruled the duel.

Award Worthy

With blazing speed and perfect aim, Denton "Cy" Young bewildered batters who could barely see the ball. Starting in 1890, Cy Young began piling up 511 victories, a record that may never be beaten. Each year, Young is honored when the Cy Young Award is given to baseball's two best pitchers.

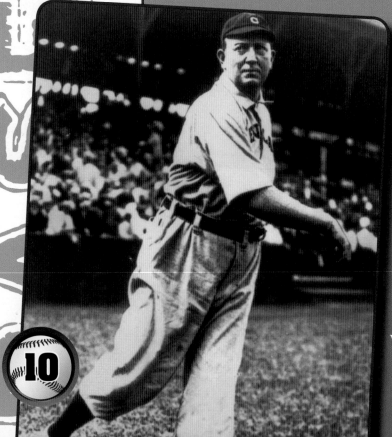

Young warms up with the Cleveland Naps before a game in 1910.

Schoolyard Hero

At the turn of the twentieth century, children everywhere had heard of Christy Mathewson. The New York Giants pitcher was the first student of the art of pitching and had several curving and sliding pitches to choose from. His control and grace under pressure, 373 wins, and 2.13 career **ERA** made him one of the first members of the Baseball Hall of Fame.

Christy
Mathewson

The Big Train

Another beloved hero was the Washington Senators' Walter "Big Train" Johnson. Johnson was a dependable winner, putting together a decade of 20-win seasons from 1910 to 1919. Johnson regularly silenced an entire team's batters, recording 110 **shutouts**, which is an all-time record.

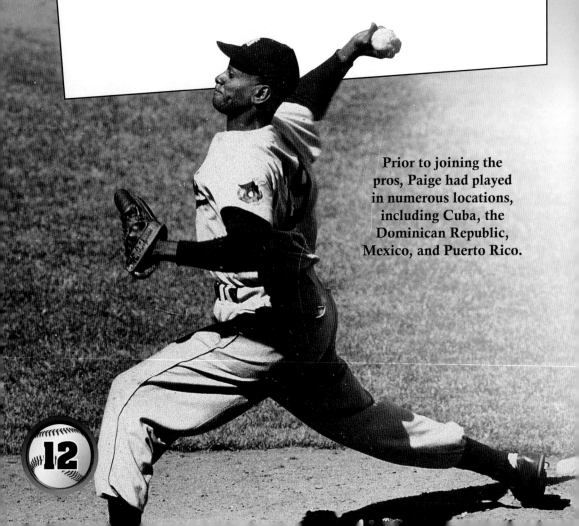

Leroy "Satchel" Paige would pitch for any team, in any league, in any country, on any night. Game after game, Paige amazed crowds and shut out teams with perhaps the greatest pitching arm in history. Unfortunately, his race kept him out of Major League Baseball until 1948, when he became the oldest **rookie** in history at 42. Despite a well-worn arm, he still had several quality games, including four shutouts. In 1971, he became the first former **Negro League** player to be voted into the Baseball Hall of Fame.

Prior to joining the pros, Paige had played in numerous locations, including Cuba, the Dominican Republic, Mexico, and Puerto Rico.

The Lovable Lefty

Although joint pain cut short the career of the Brooklyn/ Los Angeles Dodgers' Sandy Koufax, he accomplished more in 12 years than many players have in 20. From 1955 to 1966, Koufax won three Cy Young Awards, four World Series, and two awards for World Series MVP (most valuable player). Koufax was also a three-time "triple crown" winner, leading the league in **strikeouts**, wins, and ERA three separate seasons. He threw four **no-hitters**, including one perfect game, and was the youngest player ever named to the Hall of Fame.

Sandy Koufax

Southpaws

Left-handed pitchers are sometimes referred to as "southpaws." Historians believe the term came about because pitchers faced west in many early ballparks. That meant a left-handed pitcher threw with the hand on the south side of the ballpark.

Nolan Ryan introduced batters to the scariest pitch imaginable—a 100-mile (160-km) per hour fastball. The movement and speed of Ryan's pitches helped him record 5,714 career strikeouts across 4 decades—from 1966 to 1993. The speedballer threw for over 300 strikeouts in six different seasons. He also threw seven no-hitters, which is more than any other pitcher.

Not only was Ryan one of the fastest pitchers of all time, he also played for more seasons than any other player.

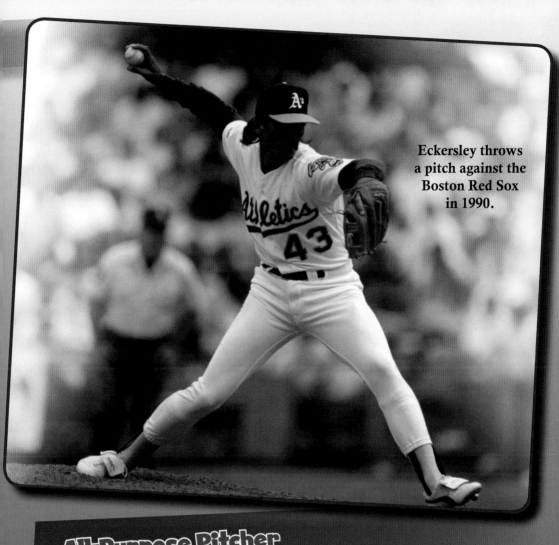

Eckersley throws a pitch against the Boston Red Sox in 1990.

All-Purpose Pitcher

When Dennis Eckersley entered the league in 1975, he was a starting pitcher with a terrifying fastball. After he went to the Oakland Athletics in 1987, the manager used his hard-to-hit heat to close out games. Eckersley's success in both roles has made him one of only two pitchers to get more than 20 wins and 50 saves in the same season.

15

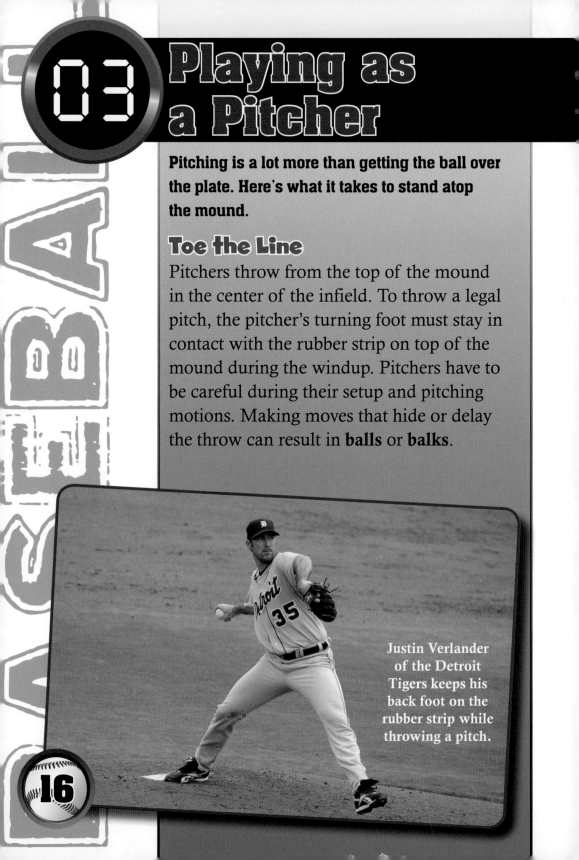

03

Playing as a Pitcher

Pitching is a lot more than getting the ball over the plate. Here's what it takes to stand atop the mound.

Toe the Line

Pitchers throw from the top of the mound in the center of the infield. To throw a legal pitch, the pitcher's turning foot must stay in contact with the rubber strip on top of the mound during the windup. Pitchers have to be careful during their setup and pitching motions. Making moves that hide or delay the throw can result in **balls** or **balks**.

Justin Verlander of the Detroit Tigers keeps his back foot on the rubber strip while throwing a pitch.

Pitchers use different throws to target certain areas in and around the strike zone in order to get the batter to miss. Even so, it's the catcher who most often decides what pitch to throw. The catcher signals for a pitch and often indicates a location as well. If the pitcher agrees, he throws. Otherwise, he shakes off, or says no to, the call. However, if the pitcher is less experienced than the catcher, he should trust the catcher's calls.

The Delivery

Overhand throws are most common and least likely to hurt the arm, but some pitchers use sidearm pitches or "submarine" throws, which are thrown underarm with an upward motion.

Pitchers and catchers occasionally meet on the mound to discuss pitches. Here, Cliff Lee of the Texas Rangers talks with his catcher, Matt Treanor.

Types of Pitches

There are many types of pitches that pitchers can use. A pitcher with multiple pitches in his toolbox has a better chance of getting a batter out.

Fastballs

A fastball is a basic pitch, delivered by winding up and throwing the ball as fast as possible at a target within the strike zone. Batters who aren't ready for a fastball may not be able to react fast enough to hit it. Good pitchers also add some movement to the ball, making it harder to hit. For instance, by putting spin on the ball the pitcher can throw a sinker, which is a pitch that drops suddenly as it approaches the plate.

The Milwaukee Brewers' Yovani Gallardo has a great slider—a fast pitch that breaks down and to the side at the last second.

High-Cost Curves

To get extreme movement on a ball, pitchers twist their arms and joints in unusual ways. The "screwballs" they throw might be effective, but they often lead to injury over time.

This picture of the Atlanta Braves' Billy Wagner shows the stress he puts on his arm when pitching.

Changeups and Off-Speed Pitches

To keep batters guessing, pitchers mix fastballs with slower pitches called changeups. Switching makes batters swing early or late. Off-speed pitches can be fast or slow, but usually deal more with movement than speed. These pitches are often thrown to curve or "break" in different directions in the air, even at fast speeds, to get batters to miss. Pitchers do this by putting spin on the ball.

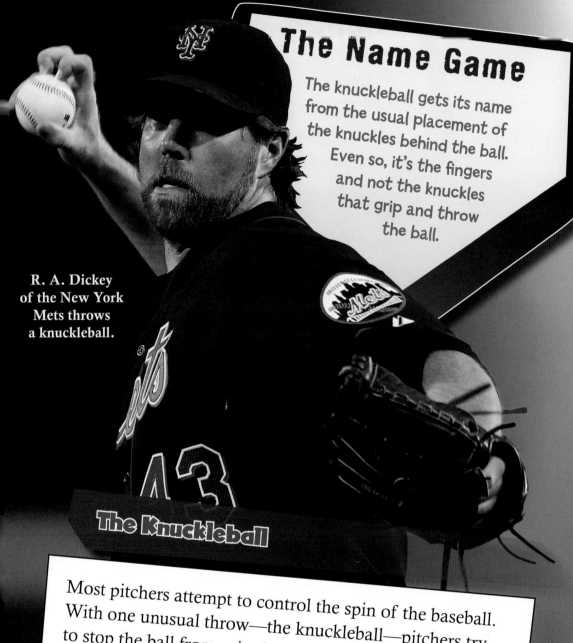

The Name Game

The knuckleball gets its name from the usual placement of the knuckles behind the ball. Even so, it's the fingers and not the knuckles that grip and throw the ball.

R. A. Dickey of the New York Mets throws a knuckleball.

The Knuckleball

Most pitchers attempt to control the spin of the baseball. With one unusual throw—the knuckleball—pitchers try to stop the ball from spinning at all. They set their fingers behind the ball to throw it flat. Not even the pitcher knows where the ball might go as the loss of spin causes it to wiggle and dance in flight.

On rare occasions, a pitcher might bring out a pitch so slow or so unusual that it might confuse the batter entirely. Pitchers who do this are said to be "throwing junk." Some pitchers use very slow pitches or "floaters" that barely have the energy to reach the catcher's mitt. Others throw an "eephus" pitch, which travels a high arc above the batter's head before dropping down into the strike zone.

Mark Buehrle of the Chicago White Sox sometimes throws the "eephus" pitch.

Key Skills

No two pitchers are alike. Their individual skills and talents determine how they can best help a team. Here are some of the ways pitchers can contribute.

Starters

The pitcher who begins a game for a team is called the starting pitcher. Teams keep a rotation of starters—a series of pitchers who start games one after another in order. Each starter plays one game and then rests a few games to keep his arm healthy. Starters usually master three or more pitches and have the strength to go at least six innings. Most well-known pitchers are starters.

The New York Yankees' CC Sabathia is one of the best starting pitchers in baseball—and the highest paid.

Relief pitcher Rafael Soriano celebrates with catcher John Jaso after the Tampa Bay Rays beat the Detroit Tigers.

Relievers

Relief pitchers are pitchers who take over for a starter. Perhaps the pitcher is getting tired or having a bad outing. Sometimes the team is so far ahead that the starter can come out. Relievers have a few pitches they can throw well, but aren't as strong as starters. If the reliever protects the lead, but doesn't finish the game, he earns a hold. If he keeps the lead until the end of the game, he gets a save.

23

Some pitchers come in for a short period when the team has a special need. Specialists could be in for one inning or maybe one batter. For instance, a left-handed pitcher might enter to throw against a strong right-handed batter. A specialist may have a tricky throw needed for a key strikeout. A setup pitcher often works the eighth inning to keep the closing pitcher fresh for the ninth. Teams must use pitchers wisely because once a pitcher is replaced, he's done for the game.

Brad Ziegler, a relief pitcher with the Oakland Athletics, uses a submarine pitching style due to an injury.

Heath Bell is a closing pitcher with the San Diego Padres.

The Closer

The closing pitcher only comes in when his team is ahead near the end of the game, usually the ninth inning. His job is to shut down the last few batters and get the save. The closer has one or two very strong pitches used to end the game quickly before the batters figure out how to hit against him.

Battling the Batter

A pitch is only good if the batter can't use it to his advantage. Here's how pitchers keep the pressure up.

Strikeouts

The pitcher's main job is to get three strikes on the batter through a combination of foul balls, missed swings, or pitches through the strike zone. If he's successful, the batter is out. However, if the pitcher throws four balls outside the strike zone before the batter gets three strikes, the batter gets a walk to first base.

Control

A batter can also get to first if he's hit by the pitch. Pitchers must use good control when throwing to the "inside" of home plate—the part nearest the batter.

The Colorado Rockies' Ubaldo Jimenez throws a fastball against a batter with the San Francisco Giants.

26

At some point, batters will get on base. Hits are fine as long as they don't become runs. With runners on, pitchers try to throw balls that are likely to become pop flies or even **double plays**. A pitcher can also try to throw out runners who lead off too far from base. Runners do this to get a head start to the next base.

As Jeff Suppan of the St. Louis Cardinals prepares to pitch, Scott Podsednik of the Kansas City Royals leads off from first base.

Intentional Walks

To pitch to a weaker batter or create force-out situations in close games, a pitcher will walk a stronger batter on purpose. Giving up a walk can sometimes prevent a run.

Pitchers can't neglect the other role they have on defense. Any time they're not touching the pitching rubber, they're another infielder. This means that they have to field or catch hit balls and throw out runners to keep them from advancing bases. It also means that they have to back up any basemen who might be fielding the hit. Any time the first baseman fields the ball, it's the pitcher's job to get to first base to receive the force-out throw.

Felix Hernandez (right) of the Seattle Mariners catches a throw from the first baseman to get Alexei Ramirez out at first.

Despite their best efforts, every pitcher throws a wild ball from time to time. If a ball goes past the catcher, the pitcher needs to charge in to cover home plate and even help the catcher find the ball if he didn't see where it went. He may also have to rush in to field a close pop fly or a **bunt**. Even on throws from the outfield, a pitcher backs up the catcher in case the throw to the plate is off.

Jonathan Broxton of the Los Angeles Dodgers moves toward home plate to catch a pop fly.

29

Measuring Success

Statistics, or stats, are often a good measure of a pitcher's ability. These are some common ways of measuring a pitcher's strengths.

Wins and Losses

A pitcher gets a win if he's pitching when his team goes ahead and the team goes on to win the game. Likewise, he gets a loss if he's pitching when his team falls behind and then loses the game. If the lead changes after a pitcher has been pulled, it's a "no decision." Any pitcher can get wins or losses.

Francisco Rodriguez of the New York Mets celebrates after getting a win against the Chicago Cubs.

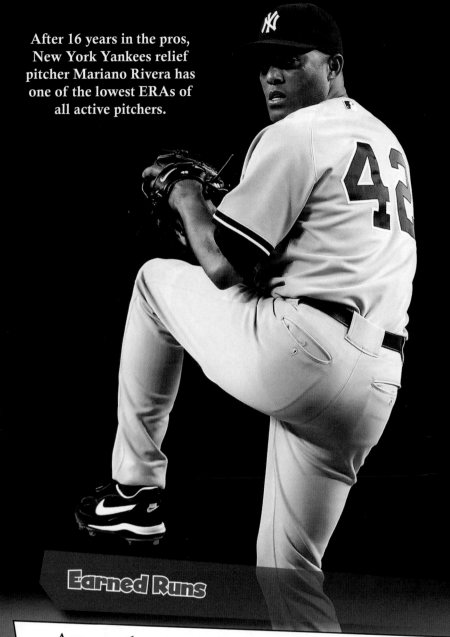

After 16 years in the pros, New York Yankees relief pitcher Mariano Rivera has one of the lowest ERAs of all active pitchers.

Earned Runs

Any run that scores under normal conditions is an earned run. A pitcher's primary stat is his ERA, or earned run average. This is a number that shows the average amount of earned runs a pitcher allows for every nine innings of pitching. The lower the number, the better.

Practice Makes Perfect

Pitchers must strengthen not only their arms and legs, but also their minds. The game plans pitchers use on batters make pitching a thoughtful position.

Pitch Masking

Pitchers want their throwing motions to be smooth, natural, and consistent. They need each kind of pitch to look the same during the windup. Hiding one's grip and using a steady delivery will keep the batter from recognizing the pitch, thus reducing his chance of getting a hit.

Tim Lincecum of the San Francisco Giants keeps his hands hidden before delivering the pitch to keep the batter guessing.

The pitcher and catcher are a team within the team. Between games, pitchers and catchers must work together to develop plans on how to beat their opponents and what type of pitch to throw in any given situation. They must also be clear on the signals for pitches. Good communication leads to a good flow between pitches, which speeds up the game and keeps batters on their toes.

Pitcher Jonathan Papelbon and catcher Victor Martinez of the Boston Red Sox celebrate a victory over the Seattle Mariners.

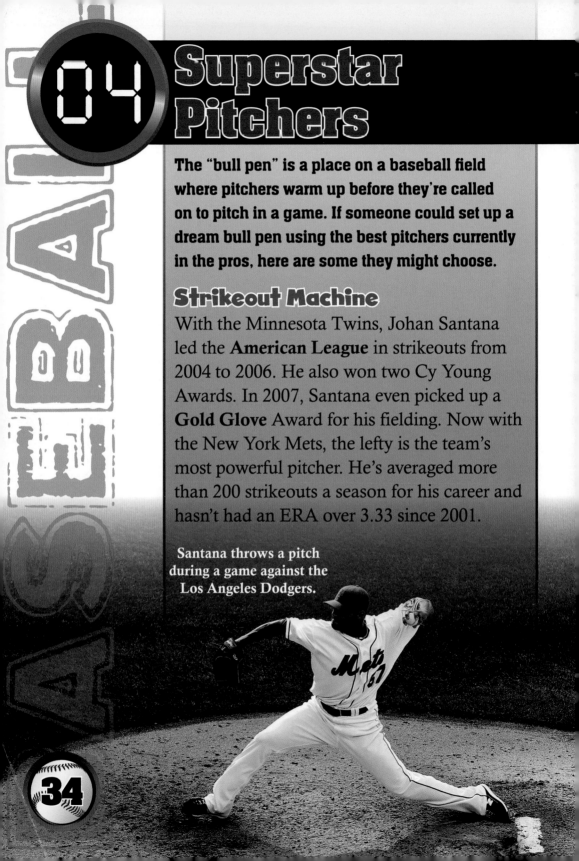

04

Superstar Pitchers

The "bull pen" is a place on a baseball field where pitchers warm up before they're called on to pitch in a game. If someone could set up a dream bull pen using the best pitchers currently in the pros, here are some they might choose.

Strikeout Machine

With the Minnesota Twins, Johan Santana led the **American League** in strikeouts from 2004 to 2006. He also won two Cy Young Awards. In 2007, Santana even picked up a **Gold Glove** Award for his fielding. Now with the New York Mets, the lefty is the team's most powerful pitcher. He's averaged more than 200 strikeouts a season for his career and hasn't had an ERA over 3.33 since 2001.

Santana throws a pitch during a game against the Los Angeles Dodgers.

At 6 feet 7 inches (201 cm), CC Sabathia looks very intimidating to batters when he's standing on the mound. His sliding curve, or "slurve," is even more intimidating. His selection of pitches and ability to remain strong late in games make him a valuable player to the New York Yankees. It also earned him three Warren Spahn Awards—an award given to the best left-handed pitcher each season.

Sabathia won a
Cy Young Award in 2007.

35

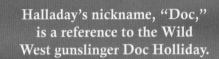

Halladay's nickname, "Doc,"
is a reference to the Wild
West gunslinger Doc Holliday.

Gunslinger

Roy Halladay combines speed
with smart placement to get
batters to hit into outs instead
of focusing on strikeouts.
His approach has paid off,
giving him 19 shutouts and
one of just 20 perfect games
in major league history. On
October 6, 2010, Halladay
pitched a no-hitter against
the Cincinnati Reds during
his first playoff game
ever. It's one of just two
postseason no-hitters in
baseball history, the first
being Don Larsen's perfect
game in 1956.

Tim Lincecum started with the San Francisco Giants in 2007. In 2008 and 2009, he became the best pitcher in the National League, leading in strikeouts and winning the Cy Young Award both years. His record of 265 strikeouts in 2008 was the best in the majors. The right-handed pitcher is unusually good against left-handed batters, helping his league-leading numbers.

Tim Lincecum

With a Capital "K"

Some have argued Lincecum's nickname, "The Freak," should be spelled with a capital K. The letter "K" is the mark used for a strikeout in official record keeping.

As the first-round **draft** choice for the Tampa Bay Rays, David Price has proven his value. His fastball regularly passes 100 miles (160 km) per hour, but he also knows how to throw the changeup. The difference in speeds between pitches confuses batters. Overcoming questions about his control, Price got off to the best start among pitchers in 2010, leading the league in wins by midseason.

Price delivers a fastball during a game against the Atlanta Braves.

Rivera celebrates onfield after helping the Yankees defeat the Philadelphia Phillies to win the 2009 World Series.

Super Mariano

In 16 years with the New York Yankees, Mariano Rivera has helped the team win five of seven World Series Championships. Considered one of the best relief and closing pitchers in the league, Mariano has closed the door on losing opponents since 1995. He has the best ERA of all active pitchers and the best ratio of strikeouts to walks. He's also an amazing defenseman, with the highest **fielding percentage** among active pitchers.

Planning on silencing some bats yourself? Try these exercises to cut down on hits by opposing batters.

The Four-Seam Fastball

For this standard fastball, position the ball so that the widest seams are horizontal across the top. Your middle and index fingers should wrap over the top of both seams with a little space between them. Your thumb comes underneath and should cross one or both seams on the bottom. Your other two fingers rest along the side of the ball. For a fastball with good upward spin, snap your wrist while holding your fingers stiff on release.

four-seam fastball

Two Seamer

To add some in-flight motion, try turning the ball so your middle and index finger each run along a seam instead of across them. Your thumb should rest on a seam underneath the ball.

two-seam fastball

Pitches go astray when the pitcher doesn't stay on target during the throw and follow-through. To practice, draw a T in the dirt in front of the pitching strip with the up-and-down line pointing at home plate. Stand with your pivot foot where the lines of the T meet. Go through your pitching motion and look where your free foot ends up afterward. It should be in line with the part of the T pointing at home plate. If it's pointed on an angle, your pitch will likely move off in that direction.

It may take a lot of practice for you to master keeping your free foot in line.

41

Never take your eyes off the ball after a pitch because it could get hit right back at you. Place one helper at first base, and pitch to another helper at home plate. The catcher should immediately throw a grounder either toward you or between you and the first baseman. If you can field it, grab the ball and throw it to first base. If the baseman fields it, run to first base to catch his throw. You can speed up this drill with a third helper throwing a second ball as the pitch arrives.

The pitcher can't afford to relax after he's thrown the pitch. He must pay attention to the ball.

An accurate pitcher can still miss a throw to a baseman if he does it wrong. Stand in a ready position on the mound where you can turn your head to see first base and third base. Don't turn your shoulders or you may get called for a balk. Turn on your foot and step toward your target. If you're working with a partner, make sure he or she is ready, or the ball will fly past, letting a runner **steal** instead of being picked off.

By picking off a runner at first base, a pitcher will make other runners think twice about taking a long leadoff.

43

Record Book

Who are the top pitchers of all time? Here are the top five pitchers in several key categories.

Career Shutouts:

1. Walter Johnson	110
2. Pete Alexander	90
3. Christy Mathewson	79
4. Cy Young	76
5. Eddie Plank	69

Career Strikeouts:

1. Nolan Ryan	5,714
2. Randy Johnson	4,875
3. Roger Clemens	4,672
4. Steve Carlton	4,136
5. Bert Blyleven	3,701

Strikeouts per Nine Innings Pitched:

1. Randy Johnson	10.61	
2. Kerry Wood *(still active)*	10.35	*(as of 9/30/10)*
3. Pedro Martinez	10.04	
4. Nolan Ryan	9.55	
5. Trevor Hoffman *(still active)*	9.36	*(as of 9/30/10)*

Roger Clemens

Randy
Johnson

Career ERA:

1. Ed Walsh
2. Addie Joss   **1.816**
3. Jim Devlin   **1.887**
4. Jack Pfiester   **1.896**
5. "Smoky" Joe Wood   **2.024**
                         2.033

Strikeouts in One Nine-Inning Game (since 1900):

1. Roger Clemens	**20**	04/29/1986
Roger Clemens	**20**	09/18/1996
Kerry Wood *(still active)*	**20**	05/06/1998
4. Steve Carlton	**19**	09/15/1969
Tom Seaver	**19**	04/22/1970
Nolan Ryan	**19**	08/12/1974
David Cone	**19**	10/06/1991
Randy Johnson	**19**	06/24/1997
Randy Johnson	**19**	08/08/1997

Seasons as an All-Star:

1. Tom Seaver
2. Roger Clemens   **12**
   Mariano Rivera *(still active)*   **11**
4. Steve Carlton   **11**
   Tom Glavine   **10**
   Randy Johnson   **10**
                              10

45

Glossary

American League: along with the National League, one of the two groups of teams forming Major League Baseball

balk: a motion that appears to be the beginning of a pitch, but does not result in a pitch being thrown

ball: a pitched baseball that passes outside the strike zone and is not swung at by the batter

bunt: the act of hitting the ball lightly without swinging the bat

double play: a situation where two outs result from a hit ball

draft: the process of selecting new players

ERA: earned run average, the number of earned runs allowed against the pitcher divided by innings pitched and multiplied by nine

fielding percentage: a measure of a fielder's ability, determined by adding putouts and assists, and dividing that number by putouts, assists, and errors

Gold Glove: an award given each year to the player with the highest fielding percentage at each defensive position in each league.

Negro League: one of several baseball leagues for African American players that existed from the late 1800s to the mid-1900s, when African Americans were allowed to play in the Major Leagues.

no-hitter: when a pitcher pitches for every inning in a complete game with no opposing batters hitting safely onto base

perfect game: a game in which a pitcher pitches every inning in a complete game with no opposing batter ever reaching base under any conditions

rookie: a player during his first year in the league

shutout: a game in which a pitcher pitches every inning in a complete game with no runs being scored by the other team

statistics: information that can be related in numbers

steal: to advance to the next base successfully without the batter first hitting the ball

strikeout: to get three strikes against a batter before either allowing the batter to reach base or to be put out by other means

strike zone: the imaginary rectangular area over the plate between the batter's knees and armpits that is the pitcher's target

For More Information

Books

Bowen, Fred. *Throwing Heat*. Atlanta, GA: Peachtree Publishers, 2010.

Buckley, James. *Baseball*. New York, NY: DK Publishing, 2010.

Christopher, Matt. *Power Pitcher*. Chicago, IL: Norwood House Press, 2010.

Dreier, David. *Baseball: How It Works*. Mankato, MN: Capstone Press, 2010.

Jacobs, Greg. *The Everything Kids' Baseball Book*. Avon, MA: Adams Media, 2010.

Lupica, Mike. *Heat*. New York, NY: Puffin Books, 2007.

Web Sites

Club MLB
web.clubmlb.com
Major League Baseball's activity-filled site has games and interactive fun features to teach kids about baseball and its past and present players.

Kids Club
mlb.mlb.com/mlb/kids
Major League Baseball's information site for kids who want to learn more about how to be a better player or want to write to their favorite player. The site also provides links to the pages of each Major League Baseball team.

National Baseball Hall of Fame and Museum
baseballhall.org
The Web site for the National Baseball Hall of Fame and Museum in Cooperstown, New York, tells the in-depth history of the game. Learn about the achievements of some of the finest players and personalities from more than 200 years of baseball.

Publisher's note to educators and parents: Our editors have carefully reviewed these Web sites to ensure that they are suitable for students. Many Web sites change frequently, however, and we cannot guarantee that a site's future contents will continue to meet our high standards of quality and educational value. Be advised that students should be closely supervised whenever they access the Internet.

Index

About the Author

Jason Glaser is a freelance writer and stay-at-home father living in Mankato, Minnesota. He has written over fifty nonfiction books for children, including books on sports stars such as Jackie Robinson. As a youngster playing youth baseball, he once completed an unassisted triple play, which is the highlight of his sports career.